# Sassy's Magic Garden
## By DeDe E. Catlin

To the real Jessica and Sassy
With love

Please send inquiries to DeDeCatlinBooks@gmail.com

"Sassy, let's go
paint a picture!"

"We can paint flowers."

"I forgot my paintbrush.
I'll be right back."

Sassy dipped a paw into
the red paint.
Ick! It was cold. She wiped it
on the grass.

Ping! A red flower popped up.
Sassy jumped in surprise.

She shook paint from her paw.
Ping! Ping! Ping! More red
flowers popped up.
*Oops! I hope I'm not in trouble for this!*

**Sassy slowly dipped a paw in white paint.**
*What if I put white paint on the grass?*

**Ping! A white flower popped up. Sassy didn't jump this time.**

She clapped her
red and white paws.
It made a new color.
Red and white made. . .

**Ping! Ping!
Two pink flowers from
two pink paws.**

Sassy wiped her paws
on the grass. Ping! Ping!
Two more pink flowers
popped up.

She dipped one paw in red
and one in blue.

She clapped her red and blue
paws and made a new color.
Red and blue made. . .

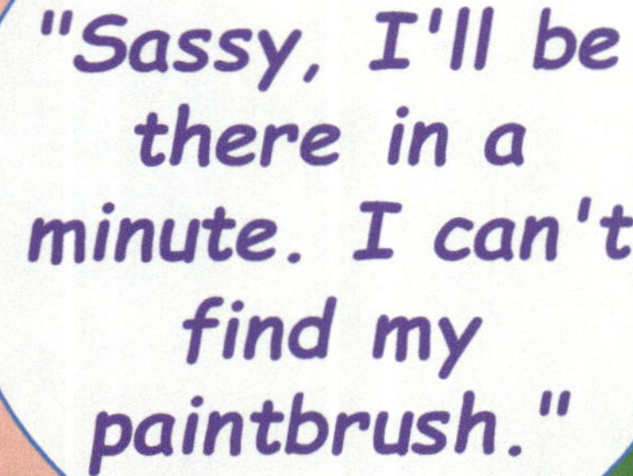

**Ping! Ping! Two purple flowers from two purple paws.**
*I hope Jess likes my flowers.*

Sassy wiped her paws on the grass.
Ping! Ping! Two more
purple flowers popped up.

She dipped one paw in blue
and one in yellow.

Sassy clapped her blue and yellow paws and made a new color. Blue and yellow made. . .

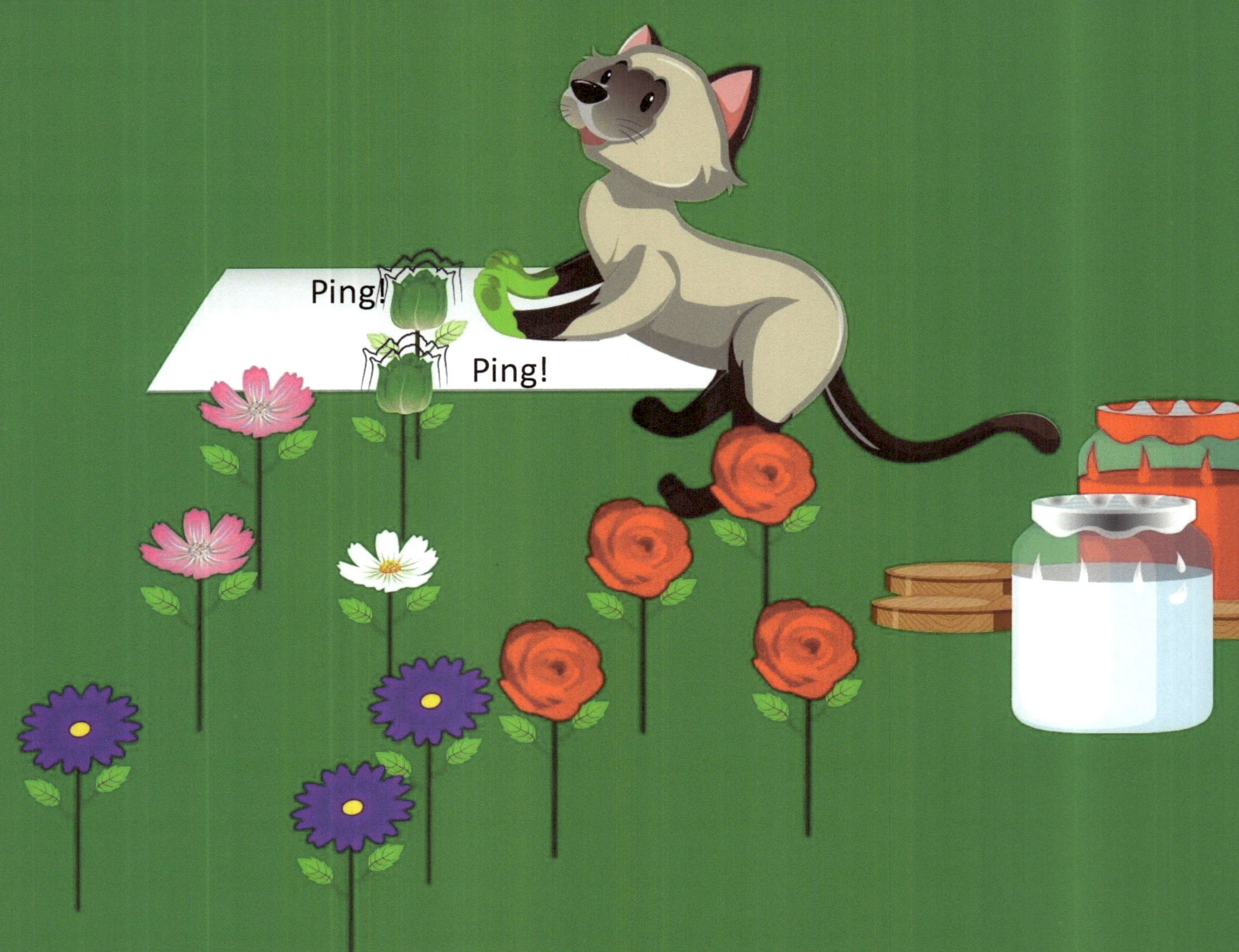


**Ping! Ping! Two green flowers from two green paws.**

She shook paint from her paws.
Ping! Ping! Ping! Three more
green flowers popped up.

Sassy dipped one paw in red
and one in yellow.

She clapped her paws
and made a new color.
Red and yellow made. . .

**Ping! Ping!
Two orange flowers
from two orange paws.**

Sassy wiped her paws on the grass.
Ping! Ping! Two more
orange flowers popped up.

**She dipped her paws
in all of the colors and then
danced on the grass.
Ping! Ping! Ping! Ping! Ping!**

"Sassy, you made a beautiful
flower garden! I love it!"

"You're so pretty. You're painted
like the garden."

*"Meow!"* **Sassy covered Jess in kitty kisses and paw prints.** *"Meow, now you match the garden too,"* **meowed Sassy.**

Dear Reader,

Thank you for reading **_Sassy's Magic Garden_**. If you enjoyed reading it, I hope you'll leave a review on Amazon. Reviews are a great encouragement to me and inspire me to keep writing. Your review will also help other readers decide if the book is right for them. If you're too young to do this yourself, just ask an adult for help.

If you would like to be notified when other books by DeDe Catlin are published, please send an email to DeDeCatlinBooks@gmail.com. You will only receive information about DeDe Catlin's books. I will not send spam or share your information, ever.

Thank you,
DeDe E. Catlin

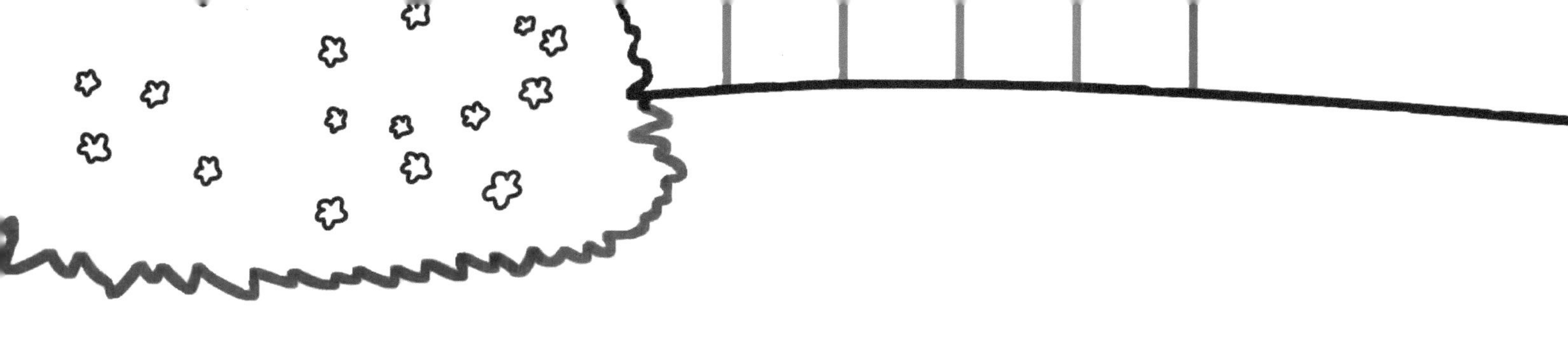

39